Kimchi

A Natural Health Food

by Florence C. Lee and Helen C. Lee

HOLLYM

About the Authors

Florence Chaeyol Lee was born and raised in Seoul, Korea. She received her bachelor's degree from Seoul National University and her doctoral degree in chemistry from Texas Woman's University. After serving as a faculty member at St. Louis University Medical School in St. Louis, she joined the Korea Ginseng and Tobacco Research Institute in 1982 where she served as head of the Laboratory of Pharmacology. Currently she is a faculty member at Seoul National University, Seoul.

Helen Chaeun Lee is presently a faculty member in the Department of Home Economics, California State University at Long Beach. She was also born and raised in Seoul. She received her bachelor's degree from Ewha Woman's University and her doctoral degree in Foods and Nutrition from the University of Illinois.

The two authors are sisters. Aside from their professional interests, they have always been involved, one way or another, with traditional Korean and other oriental cooking. Their shared interest in cooking has already produced a Chinese cookbook entitled *Ten Lessons in Chinese Cooking*. This book on *kimchi* is their second collaboration.

Copyright © 1988
by Hollym Corporation; Publisher

First published in June 1988
Sixth printing, 1995
by Hollym International Corp.
18 Donald Place
Elizabeth, New Jersey 07208 U.S.A.
Phone: (908)353-1655 Fax: (908)353-0255

Published simultaneously in Korea
14-5 Kwanchol-dong, Chongno-gu
Seoul 110-111, Korea
Phone: (02)735-7554 Fax: (02)730-5149

ISBN: 0-930878-59-0
Library of Congress Catalog Card Number: 88-83284

Printed in Korea

Contents

Preface

Korea, known to Westerners as "The Land of the Morning Calm," is located between China and Japan in the Orient. Throughout her 5,000-year history, Korea has created and preserved a unique culture comprised of the Korean language (*han-gŭl*), various folklore, unique customs, and traditional Korean clothing (*hanbok*) and food (*hanshik*).

Korea has recently emerged as a leading manufacturing and trading country with steady growth in economic strength. Korean goods are available at stores in practically every major city in the world. Korea is a booming Asian country. Furthermore, with the forthcoming 1988 Olympics in Korea, foreign travellers and businessmen are crowding into the country's airports, hotels, and restaurants as well as visiting various scenic and historical sites.

More and more people are being exposed to Korean foods, discovering the wonders of a very special Korean vegetable dish, kimchi. Once you acquire a taste for it, your dinner table will never be complete without it. A good companion dish to any meal, this vegetable delicacy may even be served as an appetizer or vegetable salad. These days you may easily buy a jar of kimchi at many supermarkets in major Western cities as well as in most Asian countries. Already, leading food companies are producing kimchi in mass quantities to meet the growing demand.

Kimchi may be classified into two main types—seasonal kimchi and winter kimchi. There are many varieties of seasonal kimchi depending on the availability of certain vegetables. In the spring, Young Cabbage Kimchi (*Haetpaech'u Kimch'i*) and Sliced Radish Kimchi (*Nabak Kimch'i*) have a refreshing taste; cool Cucumber Kimchi (*Oi Sobagi*) and Baby Radish Kimchi (*Yŏlmu Kimch'i*) are the most popular during the warm summer; for the fall season, the Whole Cabbage Kimchi (*T'ongbaech'u Kimch'i*), Diced Radish Kimchi (*Kkaktugi*), and Pony-Tail Kimchi (*Ch'onggak Kimch'i*) are favored; and winter kimchi includes Whole Cabbage Kimchi (*T'ongbaech'u Kimch'i*), Whole Radish Kimchi (*Tongch'-imi*), Pony-Tail Kimchi (*Ch'onggak Kimch'i*), and Diced Radish Kimchi (*Kkaktugi*). The winter kimchi is prepared in early winter and lasts throughout the winter until spring vegetables are available. In recent years, however, owing to the development of greenhouses, vegetables are available year round, it is no longer necessary to prepare a large stock of kimchi to last throughout the winter months.

The popularity of kimchi is attributed to the unique blending and fermentation of vegetables, herbs, pickled fish, fresh seafood, and such spices as red pepper, garlic, and ginger. Kimchi is rich in vitamins, proteins, and other essential nutrients and Koreans used to rely on it as a source of nutrients when fresh vegetables were scarce in winter.

Indeed, kimchi is recognized as a good health food. A growing number of people all over the world are acquiring a taste for it and want to prepare it themselves as they prepare their own salads. This growing interest prompted us to write this book which covers forty-eight kimchi recipes and twelve combination dishes containing kimchi, as well as detailed information about the kimchi ingredients and a brief historical account of kimchi tradition.

Florence C. Lee
Helen C. Lee

Classic Kimchi

Traditional
Whole Cabbage Kimchi

(T'ongbaech'u Kimch'i)

The traditional whole cabbage kimchi is a typical Seoul kimchi and one of the most popular in Korea. The cabbage is stuffed with a combination of aromatic vegetables, pickled fish, and fresh oysters. Here, the radishes mixed with Korean watercress and Indian mustard leaves add an aromatic taste to the cabbage, and pickled baby shrimp and yellow corvina blended with fresh oysters further elaborate the exquisite taste of the kimchi.

INGREDIENTS
Celery cabbage heads, 5
Korean radishes, 2
Green onion stalks, 5; cut into narrow strips, 2"
(5 cm)-long
Green thread onions, ½ bundle ⎫ cut in 2" (5 cm)
Korean watercress, 1 bundle ⎭ lengths
Indian mustard leaves, ½ bundle
Garlic bulbs and ginger roots, 2 each; crushed
Sponge seaweed, 3½ oz (100 g); cut into 2" (5 cm)
Pickled baby shrimp, 1 cup; chopped
Pickled yellow corvina, ½ cup; cut into julienne
Oysters, ¾ lb (300 g)
Red pepper threads
Red pepper powder, 1 cup; made pasty with water
Coarse salt, 3½ cups   Table salt   Sugar

PRELIMINARIES
1. *Trimming and Salting the Cabbage.* Trim off the coarse, discolored outer leaves of the cabbage and save them. Insert a knife through the bottom of the cabbage head, cutting down one-third of the cabbage length. Once the bottom part is cut through, split it apart holding each side. This way, the tender inner leaves will not be damaged. Soak the cabbage sections and the removed coarse leaves in a brine prepared with 3 cups of salt and 4 quarts (4 liters) of water for 3 to 4 hours or until softened. Then, rinse thoroughly in cold water and drain.

2. *Preparing the Pickled Fish Juice.* Cut the pickled yellow corvina into narrow strips; boil its juice and bones with a little water and strain.

PREPARATIONS
1. Cut the trimmed cabbage heads into 2 or 4 sections and soak them in the brine.
2. Cut the radishes into thin julienne.
3. Cut the sponge seaweed into 2" (5 cm) lengths. Wash the oysters in slightly salted water.
4. Mix the radish strips with the red pepper paste until the peppery red color is set.
5. Mix in all the remaining ingredients. Season with salt, pickled fish juice, and sugar. Finally, the stuffing is ready when the mixture is tossed with the oysters.
6. Pack the stuffing between the layers of leaves, holding back the leaves and layering the stuffing under them.
7. Firmly wrap the stuffed cabbage with the outer leaves; stack them in a crock, cover with the salted coarse leaves (PRELIMINARIES), and press down lightly.

Rich and Tangy
Northern Cabbage Kimchi

(Pukpuŭi T'ongbaech'u Kimch'i)

This kimchi originated in the northern regions of Korea. Here, a dramatic combination of cabbage and radishes and aromatic vegetables together with pickled fish creates a fanciful taste. In addition, fresh oysters and octopus lend exquisite flavors and tastes to the vegetables, and the clear beef broth used for the kimchi souse adds a subtle depth to the kimchi.

INGREDIENTS

Celery cabbage heads, 5   Korean radishes, 7
Korean watercress, ½ bundle ⎫ cut in 2″ (5cm)
Indian mustard leaves, ½ bundle ⎬ lengths
Green thread onions, ½ bundle ⎭
Dried forest mushrooms, 4; soaked and cut into julienne
Dried stone mushrooms, 4; soaked in hot water, cleaned, and cut into narrow strips
Korean pears, 2; cut into thin julienne
Chestnuts, 10; cut into slivers
Garlic bulbs, 5 ⎫ peeled and crushed
Ginger roots, 3 (small) ⎭
Red pepper powder, 3 cups; made into a paste with water
Red pepper threads
Pickled corvina, ½ cup ⎫ cut into narrow
Pickled baby squid, ⅓ cup ⎬ strips, 1½″ (4 cm)
Octopus, 1 (small) ⎭ long
Pickled baby shrimp, ⅓ cup; chopped
Oysters, ⅓ lb (100 g)
Beef brisket, 1½ lb (600 g); boiled in 5 quarts of water (beef broth)
Coarse salt, 4 cups   Table salt   Sugar

PRELIMINARIES

Trimming and Salting the Cabbage. Trim off the tough outer leaves of the celery cabbage and save them; cut each cabbage head into 2 to 4 sections lengthwise (see KIMCHI PREPARATION, page 59).

PREPARATIONS

1. Soak the cabbage sections and the radishes in a brine prepared with 3 cups of salt and 4 quarts (4 liters) of water for 3 to 4 hours or until softened. Rinse with cold water.
2. Halve the radishes, reserving 2 and make slit-cuts up to ⅔ of the length from the bottom.
3. Cut the pears into thin julienne.
4. Cut the pickled fish and the fresh squid and octopus into 1½″(4 cm)-long narrow strips.
5. Cut the 2 remaining radishes into thin julienne; mix the radish strips with the red pepper paste. Then, add all the remaining vegetables, mushrooms, and chestnuts along with the octopus, squid, and pickled fish; mix well. Finally, toss the mixture with oysters and pear strips and season with salt. This is the stuffing.
6. Pack the stuffing between the layers of the cabbage leaves; fill the slit-cuts on the radishes. Stack the stuffed cabbage and radishes in a crock; cover with the salted outer leaves (PRELIMINARIES). After 2 or 3 days, add a mixture of salt, pickled corvina juice, pickled baby shrimp juice, and beef broth, just enough to cover.

Spicy and Rich
Southern Cabbage Kimchi

(Nambuŭi T'ongbaech'u Kimch'i)

The distinctly different taste of the southern kimchi is derived from the unique blending of pickled anchovies and radishes. Furthermore, the stuffing ingredients are mixed with fresh-ground red pepper paste, thus adding a tangy taste and fragrance and an appetizingly deep, peppery-red color to the kimchi.

INGREDIENTS
Celery cabbage heads, 5 (medium)
Korean radish, 1 (small); cut into thin julienne
Korean watercress, ½ bundle ⎫
Green thread onions, ½ bundle ⎬ cut into 1½"
Indian mustard leaves, ½ bundle ⎭ (4 cm) lengths
Korean pear, ½; cut into thin julienne
Chestnuts, 5; cut into slivers
Garlic bulbs, 5 ⎫
Ginger roots, 2 (small) ⎬ peeled and crushed
Pickled anchovies, 1 cup; boiled briefly in a little water and strained—save the liquid
Oysters, 3½ lb (100 g)
Rice flour or all-purpose flour paste, 1 cup
Dried red peppers, 15; halved, seeded, and soaked in lukewarm water
Sesame seeds, 1 Tbsp
Sugar
Coarse salt, 3 cups
Table salt, 3 cups

PRELIMINARIES
Salting the Cabbage. Remove the coarse outer leaves of the cabbage and save them; cut the cabbage into 2 or 4 sections lengthwise (see KIMCHI PREPARATION, page 59). Soak the cabbage sections and the removed leaves in a brine prepared with 3 cups of salt and 4 quarts (4 liters) of water until softened, about 3 hours.

PREPARATIONS
1. Soak the cabbage sections in the brine until softened; rinse with cold water and drain.
2. Cut the chestnuts into slivers.
3. Cut the aromatic green vegetables into 1½" (4 cm) lengths.
4. Mix 1 tablespoon of rice flour and 1 cup of water and cook over low heat.
5. Crush the softened red peppers into fine pieces; add the rice paste and the pickled fish juice. Mix well.
6. Mix the stuffing ingredients—all the vegetables, red pepper mixture, pear strips, chestnuts, and sesame seeds. Season with anchovy juice, salt, and sugar; toss the mixture with the oysters.
7. Pack the stuffing between the leaves of the softened cabbage by holding back the leaves and layering the stuffing under them. Firmly wrap the stuffed cabbage with the outer leaves; stack them in a crock. Cover the top with the salted outer leaves and press down lightly.

REMARKS
When handling the red pepper powder, wear rubber gloves to avoid contact with your skin.

Refreshingly Cool and Juicy
White Kimchi

(Paek Kimch'i)

This white kimchi is much enjoyed in the northern part of Korea. The unique seasoning techniques employed—ginger and garlic strips are wrapped in a cheesecloth and the red pepper threads are used in place of red pepper powder— bring out the fresh delicate taste of a rich combination of the stuffing. Here, the juicy radishes and pears are mixed with aromatic vegetables such as Korean watercress and Indian mustard leaves as well as chestnuts, dates, and mushrooms. Rice or noodles mixed in its cold juice are a winter delight, and this kimchi goes nicely with any snack.

INGREDIENTS
Celery cabbage heads, 3
Korean radish 1; cut into thin julienne
Korean watercress, ½ bundle ⎱ cut into 1½″
Indian mustard leaves, 1 bundle ⎰ (4 cm) lengths
Green onions 3; cut into diagonal pieces
Garlic bulbs, 3 ⎫
Ginger root, 1 (small) ⎬ peeled and cut into slivers
Chestnuts and dates, 5 each ⎭
Korean pears, 2; cut into thin strips, reserving 1
Dried forest mushrooms 3; soaked in lukewarm water and cut into julienne
Dried stone mushrooms, 3; soaked in hot water, cleaned, and cut into narrow strips
Red pepper threads
Coarse salt, 3 cups   Table salt

PRELIMINARIES
Salting the Cabbage. Trim off the coarse outer leaves from the cabbage and save them; halve the cabbage heads lengthwise. Soak the cabbage sections and the removed outer leaves in a brine prepared with 3 cups of salt and 4 quarts (4 liters) of water for about 3 hours or until softened. Rinse with cold water and drain.

PREPARATIONS
1. Cut the chestnuts and dates into slivers; cut one pear into thin strips, reserving the other.
2. Cut the softened mushrooms—the forest mushrooms and stone mushrooms—into narrow strips.
3. Cut the radishes into thin strips; mix the strips with the pears, chestnuts, dates, garlic, ginger, and red pepper threads.
4. Add the mushrooms and the remaining vegetables to the radish mixture. Season with salt and mix thoroughly. This is the stuffing.
5. Pack the stuffing between the leaves by holding back the leaves and layering the stuffing under them.
6. Firmly wrap the stuffed cabbage with the outer leaves to keep the stuffing from coming out.
7. Stack the stuffed cabbage in a crock. Grate the one remaining pear and strain; mix the pear juice with salted water and pour over the cabbage. Cover the cabbage with the salted coarse leaves set aside and put a weight on top.
8. To serve, trim off the root-base and cut across the cabbage at 1½″ (4 cm) intervals. Place them in a bowl and ladle the kimchi juice on top.

Exquisite and Nutritious
Wrapped-Up Kimchi

(Possam Kimch'i)

A variety of seafood, vegetables, fruits, and nuts are wrapped together in cabbage leaves. Vegetables such as Korean watercress, Indian mustard leaves, and green onions give an aromatic flavoring to the kimchi; the fresh oysters and octopus add exquisite and fanciful flavors to the vegetables, and the pickled shrimp and yellow corvina add a subtle depth to the kimchi. Furthermore, garnishing with nuts, dates, stone mushrooms, and red pepper threads transforms the rich mixture into a festive creation. This kimchi is simply delicious and is also very nutritious.

INGREDIENTS
Celery cabbage heads, 5
Korean radish, 1
Korean watercress, 1 bundle ⎫ cut into
Indian mustard leaves, ½ bundle ⎬ 1¼"(3 cm)
Green thread onions, ½ bundle ⎭ lengths
Green onions, 2; cut into diagonal pieces
Forest mushrooms, 5; soaked in water and cut into
                 2 to 4 pieces
Korean pears, 2
Chestnuts, 5; thinly sliced
Garlic bulbs, 3 ⎫ peeled and crushed
Ginger roots, 2 (medium) ⎭
Red pepper powder, 3 cups; made pasty with water
Pickled baby shrimp, ½ cup; chopped
Pickled yellow corvina, ⅓ cup; cut into narrow
   strips (boil the bones and juice in a little water
   and strain—save the liquid)
Octopus, 1 (small)   Oysters, 1 cup
Coarse salt, 3 cups   Table salt   Sugar

Garnishing Ingredients:
Pine nuts, 3 Tbsp
Dried stone mushrooms, 5; soaked in hot water,
   cleaned, and cut into bite-size
Chestnuts and dates, 5 each; cut into slivers
Red pepper threads; cut in 2" (5 cm) lengths

PRELIMINARIES
Salting the Cabbage and Radishes. Soften the cabbage heads and radishes halved lengthwise in a brine prepared with 3 cups of salt and 4 quarts (4 liters) of water.

PREPARATIONS
1. Remove the leafy parts from the salted cabbage sections; save them for wrapping.
2. Cut across the cabbage stems at 1¼" (3 cm) intervals. Thinly slice the radish halves into a half-moon shape, then cut the slices into 2 or 3 pieces; cut the pears to a similar size.
3. Cut the octopus into narrow strips, 1½" (4 cm) long.
4. Mix the cabbage and radish pieces with the red pepper paste, garlic, and ginger; then add all the remaining ingredients, being careful not to crush the oysters. Season with salt and sugar.
5. In a medium-sized bowl, spread 2 or 3 softened cabbage leaves and fill it with the stuffing.
6. Add the garnishing ingredients on top.
7. Securely wrap the stuffing with the leaves. Stack the wrapped kimchi in a crock. Dilute the pickled fish juice with water and pour over the kimchi.

Soothingly Tasty
Parboiled Radish Kimchi

(Suk Kkaktugi)

The highlight of this kimchi is parboiling the radish cubes to derive a unique soothing taste, quite different from other radish kimchi. For an even more dramatic taste, uncooked radish cubes could be mixed with the parboiled ones.

INGREDIENTS
Korean radishes, 3
Korean watercress, 1 bundle ⎱ cut into 1¼"
Green thread onions, ½ bundle ⎰ (3 cm) lengths
Garlic bulb, 1 ⎱
Ginger root, 1 (small) ⎰ peeled and crushed
Pickled baby shrimp, ½ cup; chopped
Red pepper powder, 1 cup
Coarse salt, 1 cup   Table salt   Sugar

PRELIMINARIES
1. *Cleaning the Korean Radishes.* Select firm, white, and wholesome radishes with a slightly sweet taste. Trim and wash the radishes, cleaning the skin with a soft sponge.
2. *Trimming and Washing the Vegetables.* Trim off the leaves of the Korean watercress; trim off the roots and discolored leaves of the green thread onions. Wash them and drain.
3. *Wetting the Red Pepper Powder.* Wet the red pepper powder with enough lukewarm water to make a paste and let it stand until needed.

PREPARATIONS
1. Slice the radishes into cross sections at ¾" (2 cm) intervals, then cut the sections into ¾" (2 cm) cubes.
2. Chop the pickled baby shrimp and save the juice.
3. Cut the green thread onions and the stems of the Korean watercress into 1¼" (3 cm) lengths.
4. Parboil the radish cubes. Rinse with cold water and drain well.
5. Mix the radish cubes with the red pepper paste until a peppery-red color is set.
6. Add the cut-up aromatic vegetables—the Indian mustard leaves, Korean watercress, and green thread onions—to the radish cubes. Then add the crushed garlic and ginger and the chopped pickled baby shrimp. Mix well and season with pickled baby shrimp juice, salt, and sugar.

REMARKS
1. This radish kimchi yields no juice. Thus, for long term storage, the radish mixture should be covered with salted cabbage leaves and a weight should be placed on top to prevent possible mold growth.
2. It is always recommended to wet the red pepper powder before use in order to set a beautiful reddish color on the radish cubes and fully enrich the kimchi with the red pepper flavor.
3. Radishes grown in muddy soil are recommended for most radish kimchi; they have a slightly sweet taste.
4. The saltiness of the vegetables and seasoning ingredients as well as the fermentation temperature governs the progress of fermentation.

Refreshingly Tangy
Diced Radish and Oyster Kimchi

(Kul Kkaktugi)

The radish cubes blended with fresh oysters and pickled baby shrimp have a deep flavor and taste and are rich in nutrients such as protein, calcium, iron, and vitamins—vitamin B, C, and others.

INGREDIENTS
Korean radishes, 2
Korean watercress, 1 bundle
Indian mustard leaves, 1 bundle } cut into 1¼″
Green thread onions, 1 bundle } (3 cm) lengths
Garlic bulb, 1
Ginger root, 1 (small) } peeled and chopped
Pickled baby shrimp, ¼ cup
Oysters, 7 oz (200 g)
Red pepper powder, 1 cup   Sugar
Coarse salt, ⅓ cup   Table salt

PRELIMINARIES
1. *Cleaning the Radishes.* Select firm and hard radishes. Trim and wash them, cleaning the skin with a sponge. Do not scrub off the skin.
2. *Washing the Aromatic Vegetables.* Trim and wash the Korean watercress, Indian mustard leaves, and green thread onions. Drain well.

PREPARATIONS
1. Slice the cleaned radishes at ⅝″ (1.5 cm) intervals and cut the slices into ⅝″ (1.5 cm) cubes; sprinkle with salt and let stand until softened, about 2½ hours. Rinse with cold water and drain.
2. Cut the aromatic vegetables—the Korean watercress, Indian mustard leaves, and green thread onions—into 1¼″ (3 cm) lengths.
3. Chop the pickled baby shrimp.
4. Wash the oysters in a strainer dipped in slightly salted water, shaking gently. This way, the unique aroma and taste of the oysters are preserved. Remove shells, if any.
5. Mix the softened radish pieces with the red pepper powder until an appetizingly peppery-red color is set.
6. Add the cut-up aromatic vegetables to the red-peppered radishes. Then, mix in the chopped baby shrimp and the chopped garlic and ginger. Season with salt and sugar.
7. Toss the vegetable mixture with the oysters, being careful not to crush them. Put the mixture in a jar and press down lightly.

REMARKS
1. Fermentation progresses faster with oysters. Thus, for long term storage, it is better to leave out the oysters.
2. Pickled anchovies may be substituted for the pickled baby shrimp.
3. There are two varieties of Indian mustard greens—one is plain green and the other has a reddish tint. You may select whichever kind you prefer.
4. Wear gloves when mixing the vegetables with the red pepper powder, as it may cause skin irritation.

Peppery Hot
Pony-Tail Kimchi

(Ch'onggak Kimch'i)

Korean pony-tail radishes and aromatic vegetables such as Indian mustard leaves and green thread onions are richly blended with a paste of red pepper powder and pickled anchovy juice. This peppery preparation is a hearty delight for spicy food lovers.

INGREDIENTS
Korean pony-tail radishes, 3 bunches
Indian mustard leaves, ½ bundle
Green thread onions, ½ bundle
Green onions, 3; cut into diagonal pieces
Garlic bulbs, 2 ⎫
Ginger roots, 2 (small) ⎬ peeled and crushed
Pickled anchovies; 1 cup
Pickled baby shrimp, ½ cup; chopped
Red pepper powder, 2 cups
Rice flour or all-purpose flour paste, 1 cup
Coarse salt, 2 cups   Table salt   Sugar

PRELIMINARIES
Selecting the Radishes. Buy Korean pony-tail radishes with firm roots and fresh green leaves.

PREPARATIONS
1. Trim and wash the radishes, cleaning the roots with a soft sponge. Drain well and soak in a brine prepared with 2 cups of salt and about 3 quarts of water; allow to stand for 2 to 3 hours or until softened. Trim and wash the Indian mustard leaves and green thread onions; soak them in the brine until softened along with the radishes. Rinse the vegetables and drain.
2. Boil the pickled anchovies with a little water and cool; filter the mixture in a strainer lined with filter paper or cheesecloth, to prevent the dark-colored fish bits from getting into the kimchi souse. Save the juice.
3. Mix the red pepper powder with the anchovy juice and rice flour paste.

4. Add the green onions, garlic, ginger, and pickled baby shrimp to the red pepper mixture. Mix them thoroughly.
5. Combine the salted vegetables—the radishes, green thread onions, and Indian mustard leaves. Mix them with the spice mixture and season with salt and sugar to taste.
6. Fold the radish stems and tie with strings of the Indian mustard leaves or green thread onions. Put the bundled-up radishes in a crock and press down lightly.

REMARKS
1. This pony-tail kimchi is so named because the bundled-up small radishes resemble a pony-tail. The kimchi will be ready in about 2 to 3 days when left out at room temperature, around 70°F (20°C).
2. Fully fermented pickled anchovies—with bones softened and a slightly dark reddish color—are preferred in this kimchi preparation.
3. If pickled fish is not available, just season with salt.

4

5

6

Chessboard-Like
Radish Block Kimchi

(Sŏngnyu Kimch'i)

The radish blocks are slashed in a crisscross pattern to resemble halved pomegranates and thus they are called 'pomegranate kimchi' in Korean. This kimchi is not too spicy, yet refreshingly tasty. Favored by many, it serves as an excellent hors d'oeuvre.

INGREDIENTS

Korean radishes, 3 (medium)
Celery cabbage head, 1 (about 20 leaves)
Korean watercress, 1 bundle } cut into 1½"
Green thread onions, 1 bundle } (4 cm) lengths
Dried stone mushrooms, ⅒ oz (3 g); soaked in hot water, cleaned, and cut into narrow strips
Korean pear, 1; cut into thin strips
Chestnuts, 5
Garlic cloves, 4 } peeled and cut into slivers
Ginger root, 1 (small)
Red pepper threads
Coarse salt, 1¼ cup   Table salt   Sugar

PRELIMINARIES

Preparing the Radishes and Cabbage. Trim off the fine roots from the radishes and wash them, cleaning the skin with a soft sponge. Separate the broad and tender inner leaves from the cabbage; wash them and drain.

PREPARATIONS

1. Cut the radishes into 1½" (4 cm)-thick round blocks, reserving one-half (cut crosswise), and make crisscross slashes on the radish blocks at ¾" (2 cm) intervals in both directions. Do not cut through—leave about ½" (1 cm) on the bottom of the blocks.
2. Soak the crisscrossed radish blocks and the cabbage leaves in a brine prepared with 1½ cups of salt and 5 cups of water until softened.
3. Wash the softened radishes and cabbage leaves in cold water; drain well and gently squeeze out the remaining water from the radish slits.
4. Cut the reserved radish piece and the pear (peeled) into thin strips. Cut the Korean watercress and green thread onions into 1½" (4 cm) lengths. Cut the softened and cleaned stone mushrooms into narrow strips.
5. Mix the radish and pear strips with red pepper threads until a reddish color is set. Then, add all the remaining stuffing ingredients; mix thoroughly and season with salt and sugar.
6. Fill the slit-cuts on the radish blocks with the stuffing. Then, wrap each stuffed radish block in 1 or 2 salted cabbage leaves and stack them in a jar. Add salted water to taste.

REMARKS

1. Before serving, cut the radish piece into bite-size; ladle kimchi juice over them.
2. Pickled fish juice or pear juice may be mixed with salted water for the kimchi souse.

Refreshingly Tasty
Green Chili Pepper and Baby Radish Kimchi
(Alt'ari Tongch'imi)

In this attractive combination, the green chili peppers add an excitingly different, fragrant character to the radishes. In addition, the mini bundles of the green thread onions and Indian mustard leaves lend a subtle depth to the kimchi. This cool, tangy kimchi is a good companion side-dish to your favorite snacks.

INGREDIENTS
Korean pony-tail radishes, 1 bunch
Green chili peppers, 20
Indian mustard leaves, 1 bundle
Green thread onions, 1 or 2 bundles
Garlic bulbs, 2
Ginger roots, 2 (small) } peeled and thinly sliced
Coarse salt, 1 cup
Table salt, 2 cups

PRELIMINARIES
1. *Preparing the Green Chili Peppers.* Wash the green chili peppers, keeping the stalks on. Stack them in a bowl and put a weight on top. Add just enough salted water to cover the peppers and let them stand until they have become brownish green—for 1 to 2 weeks. Then, drain off the brine and rinse with cold water.
2. *Salting the Baby Radishes.* Buy Korean pony-tail radishes with fresh leaves and firm and hard roots. Trim and soak them in a brine prepared with 1 cup of salt and 1½ quarts (1.5*l*) of water until softened. Rinse and drain, being careful not to entangle the stems and leaves.

PREPARATIONS
1. Soak the Indian mustard leaves and green thread onions in the brine along with the baby radishes until softened.
2. Allow the green chili peppers to ferment in salted water until they have become brownish-green (PRELIMINARIES).

3. Fold the salted radish stems and leaves and tie them together to bundle them up.
4. Make mini bundles of the green thread onions — tie together 2 or 3 onions; for mini bundles of the Indian mustard leaves, tie together 1 or 2 leaves.
5. Place a layer of the baby radishes in a jar, then on top, a layer of the bundled-up green thread onions and Indian mustard leaves, fermented green chili peppers, and thinly-sliced garlic and ginger. Continue to alternate the layers of the vegetables.
6. Put a weight on top and fill with salted water to cover the vegetables. To serve, cut the radishes into bite-size pieces, or you may serve them whole.

REMARKS
The kimchi will be ready in 3 to 4 days at room temperature, around 70°F (20°C). Fermentation depends on the salt concentration of the vegetables and the brine as well as on the fermentation temperature.

Cool and Juicy
Whole Radish Kimchi

(Tongch'imi)

This is a traditional, juicy winter kimchi—a tasty combination of the radishes, Indian mustard leaves, and pungent green peppers—usually prepared 2 to 3 weeks ahead of the regular winter kimchi. The crisp radishes and the kimchi juice are quite elemental, yet deep in flavor and popular in cold winter months.

INGREDIENTS
Korean radishes, 10 (small)
Green chili peppers, 20
Red chili peppers, 10
Korean pear, 1; quartered (do not peel)
Indian mustard leaves, 1 bundle
Green thread onions, 1 to 2 bundles
Sponge seaweed, 3 ½ oz (100 g); cut into 2″ (5 cm) lengths
Garlic bulbs, 2
Ginger roots, 2 (small) } thinly sliced
Coarse salt, 1½ cups   Table salt, 2 cups

PRELIMINARIES
1. *Preparing the Green Chili Peppers.* Wash the green peppers with the stalks unremoved. Then, stack them in a bowl and put a weight on top; add a brine prepared with ¼ cup salt and 3 cups of water, enough to cover the peppers. Allow them to stand for 2 to 3 weeks—until brownish-green. Rinse them and drain.
2. *Salting the Radishes.* Select small and firm radishes. Trim and wash them, cleaning the skin with a soft sponge; roll them over the coarse salt, coating them evenly. Then stack them in a crock and allow to stand overnight.
3. *Salting the Aromatic Vegetables.* Trim and wash the Indian mustard leaves and green thread onions. Sprinkle them with salt and let stand until slightly softened. Rinse them thoroughly and drain.

PREPARATIONS
1. Roll the cleaned radishes over the coarse salt and allow to soften overnight.
2. Tie together 2 or 3 of the salted green thread onions and Indian mustard leaves, separately, to make mini bundles.
3. Thinly slice the garlic and ginger and put them in a linen cloth bag.
4. Lay the bag of the garlic and ginger flat on the bottom of a crock and arrange a layer of the salted radishes on top. Then, put a layer of the Indian mustard leaf and green thread onion bundles, fermented green peppers, sponge seaweed, red peppers, and one quartered-pear. Continue to alternate the layers and put a weight on top of the vegetables.
5. In preparing a brine for the kimchi souse—if the salt has impurities, dissolve the salt using a strainer.
6. Pour the brine over the vegetables in the crock—enough to cover them.

Summer Time
Young Radish Kimchi

(*Yŏlmu Mul Kimch'i*)

This cool, juicy kimchi is quite popular during the summer since the young radishes are readily available. In this preparation, the unique taste is derived from the blending of freshly ground red peppers, ginger, and garlic. In addition, the kimchi souse mixed with flour paste enriches the kimchi and eliminates the leafy taste of the tender young vegetables. Rice or noodles mixed with chilled young radish kimchi and its juice is a summer delight.

INGREDIENTS
Young Korean radishes, 2 bundles
Young celery cabbage, 1 or 2 bundles
Green thread onions, 1 bundle
Green chili peppers, 3
Red chili peppers, 10
All-purpose flour, 2 Tbsp; cooked with 5 cups of
water (paste)
Garlic bulbs, 2   Ginger root, 1 (small)
Coarse salt, ½ cup   Table salt

PRELIMINARIES
Salting the Cabbage and Radishes. Trim off the roots of the radishes and cabbage and cut them into 2″ (5 cm) lengths. Sprinkle the vegetables with salt and allow them to stand until softened, about 2 hours; during this time turn the vegetables over to make sure that they have become evenly salted. Since the vegetables are tender, handle them gently and do not let them become overly salted. Rinse them with cold water and drain.

PREPARATIONS
1. Cut the young radishes and young celery cabbage into 2″ (5 cm) lengths.
2. Sprinkle the cut-up radishes and cabbage with salt and allow them to stand until softened.
3. Crush the red peppers, reserving 3, into small

pieces in a mortar; add the garlic and ginger and crush them all together.
4. Seed the green chili peppers and the 3 remaining red peppers; cut them into diagonal pieces. Cut the green thread onions into 1½″ (4 cm) lengths. Then combine the salted radish and cabbage pieces with the cut-up peppers and green thread onions; add the crushed red pepper, garlic and ginger. Mix them well, carefully turning over the tender vegetables.
5. Rinse out the residual crushed red pepper in the mortar with the flour paste; further dilute the mixture with cold water, if necessary—sufficient to make the kimchi souse. Season with salt.
6. Put the vegetable mixture in a crock and press down lightly; pour the kimchi souse over it.

REMARKS
If you prefer the Young Radish Kimchi a little spicier, reduce the volume of the kimchi souce and substitute pickled anchovies for the salt.

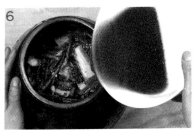

All-Seasonal
Sliced Radish and Cabbage Kimchi (*Nabak Kimch'i*)

Favored by many, this juicy kimchi is for all seasons. The thinly sliced radish and cabbage squares are elaborated with narrow julienne of aromatic vegetables such as Korean watercress and green onions. Furthermore, the fresh red pepper strips and the finely powdered red peppers exaggerate the flavor and create an appetizingly reddish color for the kimchi. It goes nicely with your favorite snacks.

INGREDIENTS
Korean radish, ½
Celery cabbage head, ¼
Korean watercress, 1 bundle; cut into 1½″ (4 cm) lengths
Green onion stalks, 2; cut into 1½″ (4 cm)-long julienne
Garlic cloves, 3 ⎫
Ginger root, 1 (small) ⎬ cut into slivers
Red chili peppers, 2; cut into narrow strips
Red pepper powder, 3 Tbsp
Coarse salt, ½ cup   Table salt

PRELIMINARIES
Preparing the Vegetables. Trim and wash the Korean radish, cleaning the skin with a soft sponge. Separate the tender inner leaves of the celery cabbage. Trim off the leaves of the Korean watercress and green onions; wash them with cold water and drain.

PREPARATIONS
1. Cut the cabbage leaves at 1¼″ (3 cm) intervals and halve the cut pieces; cut the radish into thin 1¼″ (3 cm) squares.
2. Sprinkle the cut-up radish and cabbage pieces with salt and allow them to stand until softened, about 30 minutes. Rinse with water and drain.
3. Cut the stems of the Korean watercress and the green onion stalks into 1½″ (4 cm) lengths; cut the onion pieces into narrow strips. Halve the red peppers, seed, and cut them into narrow strips; peel the garlic and ginger and cut them into slivers.
4. Add all the prepared vegetables—the green onions, Korean watercress, ginger, garlic, and red peppers—to the salted cabbage and radish pieces. Toss the vegetables thoroughly and put the mixture into a crock.
5. Mix the fine red pepper powder and a brine prepared with ¼ cup of table salt and 4 to 5 quarts of water. If the red pepper powder contains big pieces, wrap the powder in 3 layers of cheesecloth and shake in the brine to prevent any big pieces from getting into the kimchi souse and clouding it.
6. Pour the kimchi souse over the vegetable mixture in the crock.

REMARKS
1. If you like this kimchi less spicy, red pepper threads may be substituted for the red pepper powder.
2. You may try a combination of radish, carrot, and cucumber for a good color combination.

Cool and Crunchy
Stuffed Cucumber Kimchi

(Oi Sobagi)

A dramatic combination of cucumbers with aromatic leeks creates a unique taste and flavor. This crunchy cucumber kimchi, popular throughout the cucumber season, has a crisp, cool texture and serves as an excellent hors d'oeuvre.

INGREDIENTS
Cucumbers, 20
Wild leeks, 1 bundle; cut into small pieces
Green onion stalks, 2 ⎫
Garlic cloves, 3   ⎬ chopped
Ginger root, 1 (small) ⎭
Pickled baby shrimp, ½ cup; chopped
Red pepper powder, 5 Tbsp
Coarse salt, ½ cup
Table salt
Sugar

PRELIMINARIES
1. *Selecting the Cucumbers.* Select tender cucumbers of a similar size with a thin skin and as few seeds as possible. Usually, slender cucumbers have fewer seeds than fat ones; light green colored cucumbers have fewer seeds than dark green ones.
2. *Washing the Aromatic Vegetables.* Select fresh leeks; trim and wash them carefully. Avoid generating a leafy smell—do not rub the tender leaves. Trim and wash the green onions.

PREPARATIONS
1. Wash the cucumbers—rub them with salt and rinse well with cold water. Do not peel.
2. Cut the cucumbers into 3″ (7 cm) lengths.
3. Slit-cut the cucumber sections lengthwise, leaving about ½″ (1.5 cm) on both ends—make 3 or 4 slits depending on the size of the cucumber.
4. Sprinkle the cucumber sections with salt and allow them to stand until softened.
5. Rinse the cucumbers. Drain and gently squeeze

out the remaining water from the slits.
6. Cut the cleaned leeks into small pieces; chop the green onion stalks, garlic, and ginger.
7. Mix the wild leeks with the red pepper powder, green onions, garlic, ginger, and pickled baby shrimp along with its juice; season with salt and sugar. This is the stuffing.
8. Fill the slit-cuts with the stuffing and stack the stuffed cucumbers in a crock; allow to stand. To serve, cut each piece in half or serve them whole.

REMARKS
1. This cucumber kimchi will be ready to eat in about 24 hours at about 70°F (20°C). It ferments faster than cabbage or radish kimchi—thus it becomes sour sooner. Keep it refrigerated once an adequate level of fermentation is attained.
2. Triangular cucumbers are easy to work with, but the round ones will do as well. For the triangular ones, slit cut each piece 3 times; for the round ones, slit-cut each piece twice through the middle—making 4 slits.

33

Chewy   (Uŏng Kimch'i)
Burdock Root Kimchi

1. Peel burdock roots and soak them in water to eliminate the dark-colored sap. Cut the cleaned roots into thin diagonal pieces.
2. Chop green thread onions, garlic, and ginger. Prepare a glutenous rice flour paste.
3. Mix the cut-up burdock roots with the chopped garlic, ginger, and green thread onions. Then add red pepper powder, pickled anchovy juice, rice flour paste, and sesame seeds; mix well and season with salt. Allow to stand or you may serve as is.

Fresh   (Paech'u Kŏtchŏri)
Instant Cabbage Kimchi

1. Quarter one cabbage head; soak the sections in salted water until softened. Wash and drain.
2. Cut green thread onions into 1½″ (4 cm) lengths; cut red chili peppers into diagonal pieces. Chop garlic, ginger, and green onions.
3. Mix the cut-up vegetables with red pepper powder, red pepper threads, chopped pickled baby shrimp, and sugar.
4. Tear the salted cabbage leaves lengthwise into narrow strips. Mix them with the red pepper mixture; garnish with sesame oil.

Nutty (*Myŏngnanjŏt Kimch'i*)
Salted Pollack Roe Kimchi

1. Cut open the sack of pollack roe. Peel Korean radishes and cut into thin strips.
2. Cut green thread onions into 1½″ (4 cm) lengths and crush ginger and garlic. Mix red pepper powder with lukewarm water and allow to stand to make a red pepper paste.
3. Mix together the green thread onions, garlic, ginger, red pepper paste, sugar, and toasted sesame seeds; add the radish strips and pollack roe. Mix them well, seasoning with salt and put in a jar. Allow to stand.

Chewy (*Changnanjŏt Kimch'i*)
Salted Cod-Gut Kimchi

1. Rinse pickled cod guts a couple of times and cut them into 1½″ (4 cm) lengths.
2. Cut Korean radishes into thin strips and sprinkle with salt to soften; rinse with water and drain, squeezing out excess water.
3. Combine the cod guts and radish strips with chopped garlic and ginger, green onions cut in 1½″ (4 cm) lengths, red pepper powder, and toasted sesame seeds; put the mixture in a jar and allow to stand.

Salty
Sesame Leaf Kimchi
(Kkaennip Chang-atchi)

1. Wash sesame leaves and wipe dry with a cloth.
2. Mix a seasoning sauce containing red pepper powder, soy sauce, chopped ginger and garlic, red chili peppers cut into narrow strips, and toasted sesame seeds.
3. Lay sesame leaves, a few at a time, on a plate; evenly spread the seasoning sauce on top. Do the same with the remaining leaves. Place the seasoned leaves in a jar and put a weight on top. Allow to ferment to taste.

Nutty and Fragrant
Pumpkin Kimchi
(Hobak Kimch'i)

1. Halve pumpkins; scrape out seeds and pith. Cut them into $2 \times 1\frac{1}{8}''$ (5×3 cm) pieces; sprinkle with salt and allow to stand until softened.
2. Soak celery cabbage leaves and radish leaves in salted water until softened; rinse and drain. Cut the leaves into $1\frac{1}{2}''$ (4 cm) lengths.
3. Mix the salted pumpkins and green vegetables with red pepper powder, chopped garlic and ginger, diagonal cuts of green thread onions, chopped pickled baby shrimp, and pickled yellow corvina strips. Put the mixture in a crock.

36

Fresh   (*P'arae Kimch'i*)
Sea Lettuce Kimchi

1. Wash sea lettuce and drain.
2. Cut a small radish into thin strips; cut green thread onions into 1½″ (4 cm) lengths.
3. Mix the sea lettuce with radish strips, green thread onions, chopped ginger and garlic, red pepper powder, chopped pickled anchovies, and toasted sesame seeds.

Fragrant   (*Tallae Kimch'i*)
Wild Onion Kimchi

1. Trim and wash wild onions. Soften them in salted water; rinse and drain.
2. Mix red pepper powder and chopped pickled baby shrimp. Add chopped onions, ginger, and garlic; then add toasted sesame seeds.
3. Add the mixture to the wild onions; mix well. You may serve as instant kimchi.

Summertime   (*Puch'u Kimch'i*)
Wild Leek Kimchi

1. Trim and wash Korean wild leeks; cut them into 2 or 3 sections.
2. Mix the leeks with pickled anchovy juice and let stand until softened; drain off the pickled fish juice and save.
3. Mix the fish juice with red pepper powder and chopped garlic and ginger; add the mixture to the softened leeks. Mix well and allow to stand.

Refreshingly Aromatic   (*Sŏkpakchi*)
Radish and Octopus Kimchi

1. Cut radishes into $2 \times 1\frac{1}{2} \times \frac{1}{2}''$ ($5 \times 4 \times 1$ cm) pieces; cut celery cabbage into similar sizes. Soften them with salt.
2. Cut octopus, sponge seaweed, Indian mustard leaves, Korean watercress, green onions, and green thread onions into $1\frac{1}{2}''$ (4 cm) lengths.
3. Rinse the salted vegetables and drain. Mix them with the aromatic vegetables, red pepper powder, crushed garlic and ginger, octopus, and sponge seaweed. Season with salt and chopped pickled corvina. Toss the mixture with oysters.

Spicy   (*Pijimi*)
Oblique-Cut Radish Kimchi

1. Cut radishes into oblique pieces by rolling them about a quarter turn each time; sprinkle them with salt and allow to stand until soft.
2. Cut green thread onions and Korean watercress into $1\frac{1}{2}''$ (4 cm) lengths.
3. Rinse the salted radish pieces and drain. Mix them with red pepper powder until a peppery red color is set; add the green thread onions, Korean watercress, crushed garlic and ginger, sugar, rice flour paste, and toasted sesame seeds. Season with pickled anchovy juice.

Vitamin Rich (*P'utkoch'uip Kkaktugi*)
Chili Pepper Leaf Kimchi

1. Soak chili pepper leaves with baby green peppers still attached in salted water for about 3 days or until brownish green.
2. Cut radishes into thin $\frac{1}{2} \times \frac{3}{4}''$ (1.5 × 2 cm) pieces; sprinkle with salt. Cut green onions into $\frac{3}{4}''$ (2 cm) lengths; crush ginger root.
3. Chop pickled baby shrimp.
4. Rinse the salted pepper leaves and radish pieces; drain well. Mix them with the green onions, ginger, and red pepper powder. Season with salt and chopped pickled baby shrimp.

Crunchy (*Koch'u Kimch'i*)
Green Chili Pepper Kimchi

1. Soak green chili peppers and pepper leaves in salted water until brownish green; rinse.
2. Boil pickled anchovies with a little water; cool, strain, and save the liquid.
3. Mix the pickled fish juice with red pepper powder; add chopped garlic and ginger, green thread onions cut into $1\frac{1}{2}''$ (4 cm) lengths, julienned pickled cutlass fish.
4. Mix the fermented peppers and leaves with the fish juice mixture; garnish with toasted sesame seeds and red pepper threads.

Crunchy   (*Pinŭl Kkaktugi*)
Scaly Radish Kimchi

1. Cut Korean radishes into thin oblique pieces and sprinkle with salt; rinse and drain.
2. Cut Korean watercress, Indian mustard leaves, and green thread onions into 1½″ (4 cm) lengths.
3. Make a paste of red pepper powder with lukewarm water and let stand; mix with chopped garlic and ginger, sugar, and pickled fish juice.
4. Mix together the radish pieces, aromatic vegetables, and red pepper mixture.

Chewy (*Ojingŏ Muumallaeng-i Kimch'i*)
Dried Squid and Radish-Strip Kimchi

1. Soak dried squid, Korean radish strips, and chili pepper leaves in water for about 2 hours. Drain and squeeze out excess water.
2. Cut the softened squid into ½ × 1½″ (1.5 × 4 cm) pieces.
3. Mix the squid, radish strips, and pepper leaves with red pepper powder, chopped garlic and ginger, green thread onions cut in 1½″ (4 cm) lengths, pickled anchovy juice, and toasted sesame seeds. Season with sugar and salt.

Hearty   (*Yŏlmu Manŭl Kimch'i*)
Radish Leaf and Garlic Kimchi

1. Wash Korean radish leaves and cut into 2 ¾″ (7 cm) lengths. Soften with salt.
2. Cut garlic in half lengthwise.
3. Mix red pepper powder, green onions cut in 1 ½″ (4 cm) lengths, chopped garlic and ginger, chopped pickled anchovies and the juice, rice flour paste, and toasted sesame seeds.
4. Mix together the radish leaves, sliced garlic, and red pepper mixture.

Nutty (Kkaennip Kimch'i)
Sesame Roll Kimchi

1. Soften sesame leaves in salted water; rinse and drain.
2. Cut Korean radishes into thin strips and green onions into diagonal pieces. Cut Korean watercress, Indian mustard leaves, and green thread onions into 1⅛″ (3 cm) lengths.
3. Mix the cut-up vegetables, red peper powder, slivered chestnuts, and pickled anchovy juice. Place the stuffing on the sesame leaves and roll up. Put the rolls in a crock; sprinkle with pickled anchovy juice.

Aromatic (Kat Kimch'i)
Indian Mustard Kimchi

1. Soften Indian mustard leaves in salted water and rinse.
2. Chop pickled anchovies and squeeze out the juice; save.
3. Mix the pickled fish juice with rice flour paste and red pepper powder; add garlic, ginger, and green onions—all chopped.
4. Mix the softened Indian mustard leaves with the fish juice mixture, red pepper threads, and toasted sesame seeds. Make mini bundles of the mustard leaves, folding 3 or 4 of them together; stack them in a crock and allow to stand.

Spicy (Muuch'ŏng Kimch'i)
Radish Leaf Kimchi

1. Trim and wash dried Korean radish leaves; sprinkle them with salt and allow to stand until softened. Rinse and drain.
2. Mix together rice flour paste, chopped garlic and ginger, chopped green onions, pickled anchovy juice, and sugar. This is the seasoning mixture.
3. Mix the softened radish leaves with red pepper powder until a peppery red color is set; add the seasoning mixture. Mix well and put them in a crock.

Tangy (Kodŭlppaegi Kimch'i)
Wild Lettuce Kimchi

1. Trim and wash tender wild lettuce leaves and soak in salted water for about a week to eliminate the bitter taste and to become slightly fermented; rinse and drain.
2. Boil pickled anchovies in a little water and strain. Mix the fish juice with red pepper powder and chopped ginger and garlic; add thinly sliced chestnuts, sugar, and toasted sesame seeds. Mix them well.
3. Mix the fermented lettuce with the fish juice mixture.

Nutritious (Haemul Kimch'i)
Radish and Seafood Kimchi

1. Cut Korean radishes into thin 1⅛″×1″ (3×2.5 cm) pieces; mix well with red pepper powder.
2. Clean pollacks, sandfish, and octopus; cut them into the size of the radish pieces.
3. Mix the cut-up seafood and radish pieces, chopped garlic and ginger, and Korean watercress stems and green thread onions— all cut into 1½″ (4 cm) lengths; season with salt and pickled baby shrimp juice. Put the mixture in a crock.

Classic (Muu Pinŭl Kimch'i)
Slit-Cut Radish Kimchi

1. Slit cut radish halves in scaly patterns; soften them in salted water and rinse.
2. Cut radishes into thin strips; mix with red pepper powder, chopped garlic and ginger, and chopped pickled baby shrimp and yellow corvina. Add cut-up Korean watercress, Indian mustard leaves, and green thread onions.
3. Fill the slits on the radishes with the stuffing; wrap them individually with salted cabbage leaves.

Crunchy *(Paech'u Oissam Kimch'i)*
Cucumber Roll Kimchi

1. Separate leaves from celery cabbage; halve medium-sized cucumbers crosswise and scrape out seeds. Soften them in salted water, rinse with cold water, and drain.
2. Mix together chopped garlic and ginger, julienned Korean radishes, wild leeks and green onions cut into small pieces, chopped pickled baby shrimp, and red pepper powder.
3. Fill the hollow cucumbers with the stuffing; wrap them with salted cabbage leaves.

Aromatic *(Kul Kimch'i)*
Oyster and Cabbage Kimchi

1. Cut celery cabbage leaves at 2 ¾″ (7 cm) intervals. Sprinkle them with salt and let stand until softened.
2. Cut Korean radishes into thin strips.
3. Combine the cut-up cabbage leaves, radish strips, and Korean watercress and green thread onions cut in 1½″ (4 cm) lengths; add red pepper powder and chopped garlic and ginger. Mix well. Season with pickled anchovy juice and salt; toss the mixture with oysters. Put the vegetables in a jar and let stand, or you may serve as is.

Appetizing *(Shigŭmch'i Kimch'i)*
Spinach Kimchi

1. Trim and wash fresh spinach. Sprinkle with salt and let stand until softened.
2. Cut green thread onions into diagonal pieces and chop garlic and ginger.
3. Make a paste of red pepper powder with lukewarm water.
4. Mix the softened spinach with the cut-up green onions, chopped garlic and ginger, red pepper paste, and red pepper threads; season with salt.

Sweet   (*Chang Kimch'i*)
Cabbage Kimchi in Soy Sauce

1. Cut celery cabbage stalks into 1⅛″ (3 cm) lengths and Korean radishes into thin ½ × 1⅛″ (1.5 × 3 cm) pieces; soften them with soy sauce.
2. Add Korean watercress and green onions cut in 1½″ (3 cm) lengths, sliced garlic and ginger, julienned forest mushrooms, red pepper threads, pine nuts, and sliced chestnuts and pears; mix and put in a crock.
3. Mix soy sauce, water, sugar, and salt to taste; pour over the vegetables.

Peppery Hot   (*P'a Kimch'i*)
Green Thread Onion Kimchi

1. Trim off the roots and discolored leaves of green thread onions; wash and drain. Mix them with pickled anchovy juice and allow to stand until softened.
2. Mix the softened onions with red pepper powder, chopped garlic and ginger, and toasted sesame seeds.
3. Make mini bundles of 3 or 4 onions and stack them in a crock. Allow to ferment to taste.

Spicy   (*Ch'ae Kimch'i*)
Pollack and Radish-Strip Kimchi

1. Cut Korean radishes into narrow strips and mix well with red pepper powder.
2. Cut pollacks into bite-size.
3. Mix the red-peppered radish strips with the pollacks and Indian mustard leaves and Korean watercress—all cut into 1½″ (4 cm) lengths; add chopped garlic, ginger, and green onions. Season with chopped pickled baby shrimp, sugar, and salt. Let stand.

Aromatic *(Toraji Kimch'i)*
Bellflower Root Kimchi

1. Split cut each bellflower root into 3 or 4 pieces lengthwise; wash and rinse in salted water squeezing lightly to eliminate the bitter taste.
2. Quarter green chili peppers lengthwise and seed.
3. Mix red pepper powder with rice-flour paste, pickled anchovy juice, chopped garlic and ginger, and toasted sesame seeds; add the bellflower roots, green peppers, and green onions cut in 1½" (4 cm) lengths.

Juicy *(Tŏdŏk Mul Kimch'i)*
Lanceolate Root Kimchi

1. Pound lanceolate roots flat; soften them with salt. Split them into strips and wash, squeezing them lightly in cold water.
2. Cut Korean watercress and green onions into 1½" (4 cm) lengths. Cut cucumbers into 1½" (4 cm)-long narrow strips.
3. Mix the lanceolate roots with the green vegetables and chopped garlic and ginger; season with salt and put them in a crock.
4. Mix fine red pepper powder and salted water; pour it over the vegetable mixture.

Exotic *(Susam Nabak Kimch'i)*
Ginseng Kimchi

1. Trim and wash fresh ginseng roots scrubbing the skin with a brush; cut them into thin slices about 2" (5 cm)-long.
2. Cut Korean radishes, carrots, and cucumbers to the size of the ginseng.
3. Put the ginseng and vegetables in a jar. Mix a kimchi souse—1 tablespoon sugar, ½ tablespoon salt, and a few drops of vinegar to 3 cups of water; pour over the ginseng mixture. Allow to stand.

Mineral (*Miyŏk Chulgi Kimch'i*)
Seaweed Stem Kimchi

1. Thoroughly wash brown seaweed stems and cut them into 2 ¾″ (7 cm) lengths.
2. Cut Korean radishes into thin strips.
3. Cut green thread onions and Korean watercress into 1½″ (4 cm) lengths; finely chop garlic and ginger.
4. Mix the seaweed stems with the cut-up vegetables, red pepper powder, and chopped pickled anchovies; put the mixture in a crock. Allow to stand or you may serve as is.

Chewy (*Muu Mallaengi Chang-atchi*)
Dried Radish-Strips and Radish Leaf Kimchi

1. Wash dried Korean radish strips and leaves in water and squeeze out excess water; soften them in soy sauce overnight.
2. Mix red pepper powder, chopped garlic and ginger, green thread onions cut in 1½″ (4 cm) lengths, and red pepper threads.
3. Add the red pepper mixture to the softened radish strips and leaves; garnish with toasted sesame seeds. Put the vegetables in a crock and let stand, or you may serve as is.

Autumnal (*Kogumasun Kimch'i*)
Sweet Potato Stem Kimchi

1. Peel sweet potato stems; sprinkle with salt and let stand until softened. Wash them with water and drain.
2. Mix pickled anchovy juice with red pepper powder, rice flour paste, green thread onions cut in 2″ (5 cm) pieces, crushed ginger and garlic, and toasted sesame seeds.
3. Add the seasoning mixture to the salted sweet potato stems; mix well. Put them in a crock and allow to stand.

Kimchi Variations and Combination Dishes

Kimchi itself serves as an excellent basic side-dish. Yet elaborate combination dishes may be created by cooking kimchi with various ingredients, including meat, fish, noodles, and bean curd. Furthermore, the original forms of kimchi — pickled cucumbers, pickled cabbage, and pickled radishes — may be added to your list of hors d'oeuvres.

Kimchi Variations

PICKLED CUCUMBERS (*Oiji*) Short, stocky cucumbers are allowed to ferment in salted water for a week or so. You may serve these crisp cucumbers as such or seasoned with your favorite seasonings.

PICKLED RADISHES (*Muuji*) Originally started as pickled whole radishes. Nowadays, however, radishes cut into sticks are pickled in a mixture of salt, vinegar, and sugar.

PICKLED CELERY CABBAGE (*Paech'uji*) Cabbage stems are allowed to stand in salted water for a week or so. This simple preparation has a unique, fresh cabbage taste.

Savory   (*Ugŏji Tchigae*)
Dried Cabbage Leaf Stew

1. Boil dried cabbage leaves in water; rinse with cold water and squeeze out excess water. Cut into small pieces and mix with bean paste, chopped garlic, and sesame oil.
2. Slice beef into bite-sized pieces and cook briefly with the seasoned cabbage; add water and bring to a boil.
3. Add sliced bean curd, julienned forest mushrooms, green onions and red peppers cut in diagonal pieces, and a dash of glutamate; simmer.

Peppery Hot   (*Kimch'i Tchigae*)
Kimchi Stew

1. Cut pork into bite-size and marinate with a mixture of soy sauce, sesame oil, and chopped garlic.
2. Cut cabbage kimchi into narrow cross sections and combine with the marinated pork in a pot; add beef broth and a paste of red pepper powder mixed with chopped garlic and ginger. Bring the mixture to a boil; add white rice cakes (*hŭin ttŏk*), diagonal cuts of green onions, and a dash of sodium glutamate. Simmer over low heat and serve.

Appetizing   (*Kimch'i Kuk*)
Kimchi Soup

1. Cut slightly soured cabbage kimchi into small pieces.
2. Cut beef into bite-size and marinate with chopped garlic, soy sauce, and sesame oil; cook briefly. Then, add the cut-up kimchi and water and cook briefly over moderately high heat. Add green onions cut into diagonal pieces and bean curd cubes; bring to a boil. Season with soy sauce and a dash of glutamate.

Cool *(Kimch'i Naengmyŏn)*
Buckwheat Noodles and Kimchi

1. Cook beef in boiling water and cut into thin slices. Cut hard boiled eggs lengthwise in half.
2. Cook buckwheat noodles; rinse in cold water and drain.
3. Place the noodles in a bowl; pour in radish leaf kimchi and its juice. Add on top the meat slices, a slice of egg, pear and cucumber strips, and red peppers cut into diagonal pieces. Season with vinegar and mustard.

Hearty *(Kimch'i Mandu Kuksu)*
Kimchi Mandu and Noodles

1. Mix ground pork and mashed bean curd; add cabbage kimchi, green thread onions, and garlic—all finely chopped. Season the mixture with oil and salt; wrap the stuffing in round wrappers.
2. Prepare soup stock with dried anchovies and sea-tangle.
3. Cook noodles and *mandu*, separately, in boiling water.
4. Place the noodles and *mandu* in a bowl; top with kimchi and beef—chopped, seasoned, and cooked. Garnish with chopped green thread onions and toasted seaweed crumbs. Pour in the soup stock.

Tasty *(Kimch'i Ramyŏn)*
Kimchi Ramyon

1. Cut cabbage kimchi into small cross sections; boil briefly in water. Add ramyon and its soup stock to the kimchi soup; cook for 3 minutes.
2. Cut green onions and red chili peppers into diagonal pieces; add them to the boiling mixture. Then add an egg and allow the mixture to come to a boil again.

Aromatic   (*Pŏsŏt Muuch'ae*)
Mushrooms and Radish Kimchi

1. Soften forest mushrooms in water and cut into narrow strips; trim nettletree mushrooms and cook briefly in boiling water.
2. Cut Whole Radish Kimchi into thin strips. Korean radish strips softened with salt may be substituted for the radish kimchi.
3. Pan-fry the radish strips and mushrooms, seasoning with black pepper and salt. Garnish with egg strips.

Classic   (*Kimch'i Pibimpap*)
Rice and Kimchi

1. Cut cabbage kimchi into bite-size and squeeze out the juice; marinate with sesame oil.
2. Pan-fry salted squash strips, beef strips, and bracken shoots, separately; cook bean sprouts in boiling water. Season the squash strips with red pepper threads and sesame seeds. Individually season the rest of the ingredients with chopped garlic and green onions, sesame seeds, and salt.
3. Place cooked rice in a bowl; arrange the cooked beef and vegetables on top. Garnish with red pepper paste, sesame oil, and a fried egg.

Hearty   (*Kimch'i Pokkŭmpap*)
Fried Rice with Kimchi

1. Chop beef and cook, seasoning with a mixture of soy sauce, sesame oil, toasted sesame seeds, and chopped garlic and green onions.
2. Cut cabbage kimchi into narrow strips and pan-fry. Other vegetables such as squash, cucumbers and carrots may be substituted for the kimchi.
3. Pan-fry cooked rice; add the cooked beef and kimchi strips. Mix them well, frying again briefly over low heat.

Fanciful (*Kimch'i Sanjŏk*)
Skewered Pork and Kimchi

1. Mix a seasoning sauce containing sesame oil, soy sauce, chopped garlic and green onions, and sesame seeds.
2. Cut pork into ½ × 3″ (1.5 × 7.5 cm) thin strips; marinate with the seasoning sauce, reserving half of it.
3. Cut cabbage kimchi and green onions into the size of the pork strips. Arrange them on skewers in the order of pork, kimchi, and green onions.
4. Pan-fry them seasoning with the remaining sauce.

Korean Style (*Kimch'i Jŏn*)
Kimchi Pancakes

1. Cut pork into thin strips about 1½″ (4 cm) long; marinate with soy sauce, sesame oil, and chopped garlic.
2. Cut cabbage kimchi, without the stuffing, into narrow strips; cut green thread onions into 2″ (5 cm) lengths.
3. Mix a batter—1½ cups of all-purpose flour to 1 cup of water, 1 egg, and a little salt. Place one ladle of the batter in an oiled frying pan over medium heat; arrange on top the seasoned pork, cut-up vegetables, and red pepper threads. Cook until golden brown on both sides.

Festive (*Soegogi Sanjŏk*)
Skewered Beef and Kimchi

1. Mix soy sauce, sesame oil, chopped garlic and green onions, and toasted sesame seeds.
2. Cut beef into ½ × 3″ (1.5 × 7.5 cm) thin strips; cut cabbage kimchi, forest mushrooms, and green onions into the size of the beef. Marinate them all with the seasoning sauce using only half of it.
3. Arrange the pieces on skewers; pan-fry over medium heat seasoning with the remaining sauce.

Korean Style Barbecued Beef and Short Ribs

Second only to kimchi, barbecued beef and barbecued short ribs, called *pulgogi* and *pulgalbi* in Korean, are the most favored worldwide. Their rich and exquisite taste is further enhanced when accompanied by kimchi or when wrapped in fresh vegetables such as lettuce or fragrant garlands of chrysanthemum leaves.

LETTUCE WRAPPER (*Sangch'issam*) Barbecued beef, topped with red pepper paste or bean paste and sesame oil, is wrapped in a lettuce leaf—with or without rice. For an added taste, fragrant garlands of chrysanthemum leaves or green thread onions may be included.

BARBECUED BEEF (*Pulgogi*) Thinly sliced tender beef is marinated with a seasoning mixture of soy sauce, chopped garlic and green onions, sugar, toasted sesame seeds, sesame oil, and black pepper, then, barbecued.

BARBECUED SHORT RIBS (*Pulgalbi*) The meat on the short ribs is cut and spread apart without removing the bones. Then, the meat is scored and marinated for an hour or more with a seasoning sauce—a mixture of soy sauce, chopped garlic and green onions, toasted sesame seeds, sesame oil, black pepper, and sugar. Barbecue.

Lettuce Wrapper

Barbecued Beef

Barbecued Short Ribs

Barbecued Beef

Evolution of Kimchi

Kimchi and Its 2,000-Year-Old History

The origin of kimchi is believed to date back over 2,000 years. The Chinese began making kimchi around 12 B.C. In Korea, kimchi originated during the period of the Three Kingdoms, between 37 B.C. and A.D. 7. In earlier times when refrigeration was not available, vegetables were preserved with salt in order to have them available during the off-season.

Then, around the 16th century, preserving cabbages with red chili peppers became popular. As the variety of vegetables and other kimchi ingredients gradually became available, kimchi preparations further evolved into creating the tastier and more nutritious kimchi of present times, quite unique to Koreans. The different varieties of kimchi now number over 200.

Kimchi, A Good Health Food

A Natural Fermentation Product

Kimchi is a natural food created by the lactic acid fermentation of cabbages and radishes as major vegetables and of various blending ingredients—aromatic vegetables, seafood, and pickled fish. Since kimchi is rich in vitamins, minerals, and proteins, Koreans used to rely on it as a source of nutrients when fresh vegetables were scarce in winter.

Ginger, Garlic, and Red Peppers These three spices constitute the basic seasonings of kimchi—almost indispensable.

The key points in producing the best tasting kimchi are the salt concentration and the fermentation temperature. A salt concentration of 3% and a fermentation temperature around 40°F (5°C) are the most appropriate fermentation conditions which require a fermentation period of 30-60 days.

The vitamins present in kimchi are of great nutritional value and lactic ferments seem to prevent the kimchi vitamins from breaking down as the fermentation progresses until the lactic ferments reach a certain high level of acidity (over 1% in lactic acid). The vitamin contents, especially the

vitamin C level, are rather high comprising approximately 12-19 mg per 100 g of kimchi at its best, much of it being derived from the red peppers. The vitamin B_1, B_2, and B_{12} contents in particular may be slightly lower at an early stage of fermentation, but they appear to increase as the fermentation progresses, reaching the highest level (twice the initial level) when kimchi possesses the most pleasing taste.

Furthermore, a nutritional balance is maintained by presence of pickled fish and fresh seafood such as octopus, squid, and oysters which provide abundant proteins yielding amino acids, especially the essential ones. Chili peppers mask the fishy smell of the pickled fish and appear to prevent the deterioration of lipids in pickled fish and fresh seafood. In addition to lactic acid, other organic acids such as malic, tartaric, and succinic acid are also present in kimchi; yet kimchi is classified as an alkali-forming food because of its high level of minerals such as calcium and iron. The combined effects of these nutrients seem to help normalize the metabolic system and also reduce the occurrence of disorders in the digestive system.

Thus kimchi is recognized as a good health food and is rapidly gaining popularity for its taste as well as for its nutritional value.

(for 100g)

Vitamins	VITAMINS IN KIMCHI	
	Whole Cabbage Kimchi	Radish Kimchi
A (i.u.)	492	946
B_1 (mg)	0.03	0.03
B_2 (mg)	0.06	0.06
C (mg)	12.0	10.0
Niacin (mg)	2.1	5.8

Kimchi Ingredients

Kimchi is generally classified into two kinds. One is seasonal kimchi — each kimchi is named for a certain fresh vegetable readily available during that season, and thus it is for short-term storage. The other kind, winter kimchi — called *kimjang* kimchi meaning "stored kimchi" — is for long-term storage to last through the cold winter months when fresh vegetables are not as readily available as in other seasons.

Usually cabbages and radishes are the major vegetables, and aromatic vegetables such as Korean watercress, Indian mustard leaves, and green onions are mixed with them. For seasoning, garlic, ginger, chili peppers (red and green), pickled fish, and fresh seafood are used.

CABBAGES

There are two varieties of cabbage — a native variety called the Korean cabbage and a new variety, celery cabbage. The Korean cabbage has long, thin stalks; its root is larger than that of the celery cabbage and has a nutty taste. The celery cabbage head is oblong-shaped and much stockier than the Korean variety with rounded leaves on thick stalks; it has a small root with a slightly sweet taste.

The protein contents in cabbage are higher than in many other vegetables, and a significant amount of vitamin C and minerals is also found in the cabbage. Furthermore, its green leaves are rich in vitamin A. Thus, it is recommended that you eat the green leaves along with the white parts (stalks) to take in all the available nutrients.

Celery Cabbage Select cabbage heads of medium size densely packed with fresh and tender, pale green leaves.

Radishes Select firm radishes. Irregular indentations on the skin appear to serve as a fair indication of hardness.

RADISHES

There are three kinds of radishes: a native variety called the Korean radish, the Japanese radish which originated from Japan, and the Korean native pony-tail radish. Korean radishes have a firm, stumpy root with rootlets and rounded ends; they are used for Diced Radish Kimchi and Whole Radish Kimchi and also for the stuffing of many kinds of cabbage kimchi. The Japanese variety is long and slim with a rather pointed end and has almost no rootlets; they are used for Sweet-and-Salty Radish Kimchi or Radish Pickles. Pony-tail radishes have a firm, stocky small root which tapers down toward the top of the root; they are used for Baby Radish Kimchi and Pony-Tail Kimchi. Tender stalks and leaves of young spring radishes are used for Young Radish Kimchi.

The taste of a single radish root also varies somewhat depending on the part of the root. That is, the upper part where stalks are attached is not as tangy as the rest; the middle part is slightly sweet and good for shredded radish dishes; and the bottom part is most tangy and thus used for Diced Radish Kimchi.

Radish roots are rich in vitamins and diastase which promotes the digestion of carbohydrates. Vitamin C, calcium, and carotenes are also found in radish stalks and leaves.

GREEN ONIONS

Green onions are used in many recipes for their flavor and taste. Almost no kimchi is complete without green onions.

There are two varieties — a native variety, green

Indian Mustard Greens There are two varieties — one with plain green leaves and the other with reddish green leaves. The more intense the color is, the stronger the fragrance.

thread onions and a new variety, a much larger species which originated in China. Green thread onions have a unique poignant taste, are firm and do not spoil readily. Thus, they are used for winter kimchi as well as for Green Thread Onion Kimchi itself. On the other hand, the new Chinese variety spoils easily due to too much sap on the underside of the large dark green leaves; so it is usually used for short-term storage kimchi.

Select firm and fresh green onions which have a good deal of white stalk and not too much dark green leaf parts. They are rich in vitamins and minerals, especially calcium.

KOREAN WATERCRESS

This Korean native watercress, rich in vitamins A and C and calcium, is widely used for just about all kinds of kimchi, largely because of its invitingly rich aromatic flavor.

Fresh watercress has plump stalks with lots of leaves and preferably with roots still unremoved. Its fresh tender leaves and stems with a slightly reddish tint exert a stronger aroma than the plain green ones.

INDIAN MUSTARD LEAVES

Indian mustard leaves are rich in vitamins A and C and minerals such as calcium and iron and are thus recognized as a good health food. They are widely used in various kimchi preparations besides the Mustard Kimchi itself.

There are two varieties—one is plain green and

the other has a slightly reddish tint. The stronger the color of the leaves is, the sharper the aroma is; thus you should select whichever you would prefer. In general, leaves with a reddish tint are used for Whole Cabbage Kimchi or Radish Kimchi, while plain green ones are used for White Kimchi or the like which requires a crisp clear appearance.

SPONGE SEAWEED

This seaweed has a unique aroma and lends a cool and crispy taste to kimchi. It can be bought fresh or dried. Fresh seaweed should be full, shiny, and green, while the dried ones should be light green and free of contaminants.

It is rich in calcium and iodine and also known to be helpful in preventing heart ailments.

RED AND GREEN CHILI PEPPERS

Red chili peppers add a poignant taste and an appetizingly attractive color to kimchi. Of the two kinds available, the native variety is hotter with tender skin and more seeds and is smaller than the other variety which originated in China. The Chinese variety is much larger and has a thick skin, thus yielding more powder when ground.

Red peppers are rich in vitamins A (carotenes), B, and C. The vitamin C contents are especially higher than in many other vegetables. Naturally sun-dried red peppers with a bright and shiny red color retain their poignant flavor and hot taste better than those dried employing modern technology.

Red chili peppers cut into thin strips—red pepper threads—are also widely used for both taste and decoration, especially in Wrapped-Up

Korean Watercress Korean native watercress has plump stalks with many leaves and is rich in vitamins A and C.

Kimchi, White Kimchi, and Sliced Cabbage and Radish Kimchi.

Unripened green chili peppers are also used in kimchi preparations such as Green Pepper Kimchi, Green Chili Pepper and Baby Radish Kimchi, and Whole Radish Kimchi. However, for flavoring and blending in kimchi preparations, green peppers are usually used in combination with red peppers.

GARLIC
Garlic is a well-recognized health food and appears to help normalize the digestive system and exert anaesthetic and antibactericidal effects. Furthermore, this highly aromatic garlic has been the subject of studies for its anticarcinogenic effects.

Six-cloved garlic bulbs, recognized as the top grade, have firm, hard cloves, each with a well-defined shape and a furrow between the cloves. Medium-sized bulbs with shiny skin distinctive in its texture are strongly aromatic and have a sharp taste. Large ones lack the same sharp taste.

GINGER
This aromatic root is used for its piercing taste and flavor as well as for masking unwanted tastes. Better roots are larger with fewer nodes and have a very thin, almost transparent skin; when you break the root between the nodes with your fingers, the texture should not be stringy.

SALT
Salt concentration governs the taste of food. When kimchi is too salty, the true fresh and aromatic

Red Peppers Naturally sun-dried peppers are bright and shiny red and have a very poignant flavor.

taste of the kimchi will be lost. Therefore, care must be taken to use an appropriate amount of salt in softening the vegetables and also in seasoning the kimchi ingredients. Furthermore, unnecessarily salty food is harmful to your system.

Coarse salt is used in softening vegetables, while white table salt is used in seasoning and souse preparation.

PICKLED BABY SHRIMP
Good pickled baby shrimp is pinkish and its juice is greyish-white. Both chopped baby shrimp and its juice are used for seasoning and for the kimchi souse.

PICKLED ANCHOVIES
Silverish maroon-colored pickled anchovies may be used as is when fully fermented, or they may be boiled with the juice and a little water. The liquid is then used after it has been strained — for seasoning and for kimchi souse. The bones and meat are chopped and used in kimchi preparations such as Diced Radish Kimchi or the like.

PICKLED CORVINA
Usually the pickled fish is filleted and the fillets are cut into narrow strips for seasoning. The remainder is boiled with the juice and a little water; the liquid is strained through cheesecloth or filter paper and used for the kimchi souse.

PICKLED YELLOW CORVINA
For kimchi seasoning, this pickled fish is usually filleted and the fillets are cut into strips. The remainder and the juice are boiled with added water; the liquid, after being strained, is used for the kimchi souse.

Garlic Each clove should have a well-defined shape with shiny skin distinctive in its texture.

Kimchi Preparation I

The proper cutting of the basic kimchi vegetables and seasoning ingredients including pickled fish and fresh seafood is an important part of kimchi preparation. A large variety of vegetables are cut into different shapes and sizes for use in a number of kimchi preparations.

Cutting Techniques

1. **Celery Cabbage Strips** Tear the cabbage leaves into strips.

2. **Cabbage Slices** Cut the leaves at 1¼″ (3 cm) intervals.

3. **Korean Radish Squares** Cut the radishes into thin 1¼″ (3 cm) squares.

4. **Radish Cubes** Cut the radishes into ¾″ (2 cm) cubes.

5. **Round Radish Slices** Slice the radishes into thin round pieces.

6. **Half-Moon Slices** Slice halved-radishes into thin cross sections.

7. **Quartered Slices** Slice quartered-radishes into thin cross sections.

8. **Radish Sticks** Cut the radishes into ⅜×1½″ (1×4 cm) thin sticks.

9. **Radish Julienne** Cut the thin round pieces into narrow strips.

10. **Scored Radish Halves** Score scaly patterns on radish halves.

11. **Crisscrossed Radish Blocks** Score at ⅜″ (2 cm) intervals.

12. **Oblique Cuts** Cut and roll the radish a quarter turn each time.

13. **Chopped Pickled Baby Shrimp** Drain the juice and chop.

14. **Diagonal Cuts of Green Onions** Cut the onions at 45-60° angles.

15. **Bite-Size Fish Cuts** Fillet the fish and cut into bite-size.

Kimchi Preparation II

Step-by-Step Kimchi Preparation

The taste of kimchi varies from region to region depending on the method of preparation and on the ingredients used; each family creates a unique taste. The following description is for the preparation of Seoul Kimchi—for storing over the winter.

1. **Trimming** Trim off coarse leaves and cut through the bottom.

2. **Quartering or Cutting in Half** Split apart the cabbage heads.

3. **Preparing Salted Water** Remove impurities with a strainer.

4. **Softening the Cabbage Sections** Soak the sections in salted water.

5. **Washing the Cabbage** Rinse the salted cabbage sections and drain.

6. **Washing the Baby Shrimp** Wash in a basket lowered in water.

7. **Washing the Oysters and Sponge Seaweed** Wash in salted water.

8. **Cutting the Aromatic Vegetables** Cut into 2″ (5 cm) lengths.

9. **Preparing Seasonings** Crush ginger and garlic. Make a red pepper paste.

10. **Setting a Peppery Color** Mix radish strips with red pepper paste.

11. **Mixing the Stuffing** Combine the vegetables, garlic, and ginger.

12. **Seasoning** Add fresh seafood and season with pickled fish and salt.

13. **Stuffing the Cabbage** Pack the cabbage with stuffing material and wrap with outer leaves.

14. **Putting the Cabbage in a Crock** Stack the stuffed cabbage in a crock.

15. **Adding Salt** Cover with coarse outer leaves set aside and sprinkle salt on top.

Kimchi Tradition

Many years ago, Koreans adopted several methods of preserving fresh vegetables to store them away for the winter season. Thus during the winter time when fresh vegetables were scarce, kimchi used to serve as a main source of essential nutrients such as vitamins, proteins, and minerals. In late fall and early winter, a huge stock of fresh cabbage and radishes is put away as kimchi to last until spring vegetables are available. This yearly ritual is called *kimjang* in Korean, meaning kimchi-storing.

WINTERIZATION

Winter in Korea is quite cold and lasts from three to four months. Thus, each household needs to prepare for winter, especially food and heating materials to last the whole winter through. The preparation of food usually starts with the gathering of kimchi ingredients in early summer. For instance, red chili peppers, garlic, and pickled fish are obtained during their season long before the cabbage and radishes arrive at the *kimjang* markets. Other green vegetables including green onions and Indian mustard leaves are obtained between late fall and early winter, usually about the time when the cabbage and radishes are being harvested.

Varieties of winter kimchi include Whole Cabbage Kimchi, which is prepared by stuffing the cabbage heads with seasoned radish strips;

Cabbage Market Huge piles of celery cabbage are awaiting customers.

***Kimjang* Market Place** In early winter, temporary *kimjang* markets are set up for bulk sales.

Wrapped-Up Kimchi, which consists of seasoned vegetables wrapped in cabbage leaves; White Kimchi, without red pepper powder; Pony-Tail Kimchi; Radish Cube Kimchi; and so on. In addition, there are other varieties of kimchi unique to certain regions and to certain families — such as Indian Mustard Leaf Kimchi, Radish Leaf Kimchi, and Squash Kimchi.

STOCKING GARLIC, RED AND GREEN CHILI PEPPERS, AND PICKLED FISH

Of the ingredients needed for *kimjang*, there are certain items which may be obtained and prepared much ahead of the *kimjang* season. Garlic, chili peppers, and pickled fish are some of them. If you buy them in season, you will have a good selection, and they will be much less expensive.

Red and Green Chili Peppers Red chili peppers are called for in many Korean recipes besides kimchi. During early summer, green chili peppers are available and later in September the green ones ripen to red. Then, the red peppers are sun dried and pulverized or cut into threads, while some are kept whole and stored away to use for *kimjang* and also to use until the next fresh batches are available.

Dried red peppers should be stored in the shade with good ventilation. Once the peppers are ground, the powder should be kept in an airtight container in the freezer to prevent any quality change, or it may be left out when it is well dried and mixed with salt to prevent deterioration and the invasion

Radish Market Stacks of fresh radishes are a joyous scene — the splendor of bounty.

of insects.

Garlic Garlic cloves are usually planted in the fall and harvested the following summer, around June. Garlic comes in a bundle of 100 bulbs, arranged by their stalks on straw braids. Good quality garlic has six cloves in each bulb, and each clove is firm and hard and has a well-defined shape; it wears multilayers of shiny skin distinctive in its texture. Store them in a cool, shady place with good ventilation.

Pickled Fish Fresh seafood such as shrimp, anchovies, and corvina (with intestines) are salted and allowed to ferment. During fermentation, the fish protein is broken down to amino acids and thus a unique aroma is produced. The most commonly used pickled fish for winter kimchi include baby shrimp, anchovies, corvina, and yellow corvina. Depending on the season, there are several grades of pickled shrimp, including May, June, and Fall grades. For winter kimchi (*kimjang* kimchi), the June grade is favored since the shrimp are full and saltier than other grades. Good pickled baby shrimp are pinkish without impurities and their juice is greyish-white. Silverish maroon-colored pickled anchovies of medium size, prepared in June, are the best in quality; nowadays their juice is available in bottles. Corvina is pickled between mid-May and mid-June. When you prepare it yourself, select fresh corvina with bright red gills, shiny scales, and bright and intensely colored skin; this pickled fish tastes best when it is pickled in plenty of juice, and the meat should look slightly yellow when fully fermented. Pickled yellow corvina is usually prepared between the months of May and June; clean them thoroughly and sprinkle them with plenty of salt. Put the salted fish in a crock, seal airtight, and allow to stand until fully fermented.

WHERE TO BUY?

During the *kimjang* season, starting in November, most of the market places are dominated by *kimjang* materials and additional temporary markets are installed on empty lots. Huge piles of cabbage heads and radishes await customers in one corner and piles of Indian mustard leaves, Korean watercress, red chili peppers, garlic, ginger, and other necessary items are found in other corners. For those who have not prepared certain ingredients necessary for *kimjang*, this is a second opportunity to buy them.

The *kimjang* markets last through the middle of December. By then, most Koreans are done with *kimjang*. Imagine what an enormous amount of vegetables are stored away during this one-month period.

THE SIZE OF *KIMJANG*

In olden times, when the size of an average family was rather large, three generations living under the same roof, the amount of cabbage used was between 70 and 100 heads, weighing about 4½ lb (2 kg) each. Nowadays, however, many one-family units have been reduced to nuclear families, and the quantity of cabbage and radishes per family are accordingly reduced to only about 20 to 25 heads and 10 to 15 radishes weighing 1¾ lb (800 g) each. Furthermore, recent changes in meal patterns toward Western style have also contributed to

Green Onion Market Green onions and green thread onions are widely used for their flavor and taste.

61

the reduction in the amount of *Kimjang*.

The preparation of the vegetables for winter, *kimjang*, is a cooperative work by relatives or friendly neighbors. It requires a great deal of work, and one person is in no way able to manage all that load of work in a day or so. You simply need helping hands, and it is a time when the friendly Korean nature is expressed. It is a beautiful Korean tradition.

WHAT A TASTE!

The unique taste of kimchi vary depending on the main vegetables used (whether cabbage, radishes, sesame leaves, or Indian mustard leaves), on the contents of the stuffing material with its many variations, and on the proportion of the ingredients used—including pickled fish, aromatic vegetables, and seasoning material. Thus, Whole Cabbage Kimchi is refreshingly tangy; Radish Kimchi, cool and juicy; Cucumber Kimchi, rich in fragrance and crunchy; Green Chili Pepper Kimchi, crisp and tart; and Sesame Roll Kimchi, nutty—to mention just a few.

The taste of kimchi also varies from region to region within the country. In the north where the weather is rather cool, the kimchi is less salty and plain with more of a fresh vegetable taste than the southern variations. On the other hand, in the southern part of the country, where the weather is

Pickled Fish Market Pickled baby shrimp, anchovies, corvina, and yellow corvina are usually used for winter kimchi.

Traditional New Year's Day Dinner Table Cabbage Kimchi, Sliced Radish and Cabbage Kimchi, and Wrapped-Up Kimchi constitute the basic side-dishes.

much warmer, more salt is added along with pickled fish, and the kimchi is less juicy and richer in flavor.

The exquisite taste of kimchi is set when the fermentation reaches a certain level at which an adequate amount of lactic ferments has been produced. The lactic ferments create a refreshingly cool taste which enhances one's appetite.

In Korea, no dinner table is complete without kimchi; kimchi constitutes a very basic side-dish for any meal and serves as an excellent hors d'oeuvre. In addition, dishes prepared in combination with kimchi are numerous—Kimchi Stew, Kimchi Soup, Fried Rice and Kimchi, Kimchi *Mandu*, and many more. Even overly fermented kimchi may be used for combination soups or dishes.

Kimchi goes nicely with any Western cuisine as well as Japanese or Chinese food.

KIMCHI, A STAMINA BUILDER

Kimchi is rich in protein and vitamins, especially vitamins B and C and also contains various minerals such as calcium and iron. Pickled fish and

62

have all the nutrients well preserved. Therefore, the amount of salt used for softening the vegetables, for seasoning, and for the kimchi souse must be properly adjusted; the storage temperature should be well controlled throughout the season to avoid over fermentation and thus souring.

To avoid temperature fluctuations during storage, winter kimchi used to be stored underground in crocks; the crocks, filled with kimchi, were covered with straw mats, then by dirt. It is always recommended to store kimchi in a number of small crocks rather than in one large crock. Since kimchi will be taken out frequently, it is necessary to minimize disturbances to avoid temperature fluctuations. The underground temperature is supposedly maintained at 40-50°F (5-10°C) throughout the winter. This temperature-controlling method is still widely practiced in rural areas and among city dwellers who have enough yard ground to accommodate a couple of crocks. For apartment dwellers, containers filled with chaff or sawdust are used to achieve a similar effect. In recent years, however, Styrofoam containers designed for kimchi storage have been widely used.

Care must be taken when taking the kimchi out of the crock not to cause unnecessary disturbance; thus, afterwards, always re-cover the vegetables, pressing down lightly with the cabbage leaves used as the cover. Proper handling minimizes further fermentation and possible mold formation.

various fresh seafood are a source of minerals and provide a substantial amount of protein which yields amino acids during fermentation. The salt in kimchi appears to promote the breakdown of protein to amino acids, thus increasing the amount of essential amino acids which serve as building blocks in the system but must be taken in. Therefore, kimchi used to be the main source of nutrients during the winter season when fresh vegetables were not readily available. Kimchi also contains a large amount of garlic which is known to normalize the digestive system and to help reduce fatigue and build stamina. Garlic also has been the subject of intense studies for its anticarcinogenic effects.

Hence, kimchi has been recognized in recent years as a good health food as well as a stamina builder.

KIMJANG (STORING-KIMCHI)

Kimjang is a means of storing kimchi to last the winter season, three to four months, during which time fresh vegetables are not readily available. Here, the utmost concerns for tasty kimchi are the fermentation conditions — the salt concentration and the fermentation temperature — to produce an adequate amount of ferments and to

Crocks for Winter Kimchi Storage To avoid temperature fluctuations, winter kimchi is stored in crocks seated underground.

63